A Santhali Grammar

Madhusudan Mishra

SHIPRA

ISBN : 81-7541-285-2

First Published in India in 2006

A Santhali Grammar

Published by:
SHIPRA PUBLICATIONS
115-A, Vikas Marg, Shakarpur, Delhi-110092, INDIA
Phone: 91-11-55277210, 91-11-22500954
Fax: 91-11-22458662
E-mail: info@shiprapublications.com
www.shiprapublications.com

Preface

This Santhali Grammar is exclusively based on the linguistic material presented by Bodding in his Santhal dictionary. I have never been personally in contact with the Santhali speaking people. Therefore, this grammar, based on secondary source, may require correction and improvement here and there.

Even some points of comparison with the Bihari dialects may be questionable. I shall gladly welcome every criticism of the dialect-experts and of the native speakers of all the dialects including Santhali. I speak only one of the Bihari dialects, though I have been in touch with all of them.

I have not also seen any grammar of Santhali and, I am afraid, some points of grammar may be missing.

Though Bodding has not distinguished the short and long vowels of Santhali in his dictionary, it has been done in this grammar as far as verifiable from the Bihari dialects. The distinction of short and long vowels is perhaps not phonemic. Therefore, this uncertainty may be put up with as far as tolerable.

Needless to say, any criticism will be gratefully welcomed, because later it may increase the value of the book.

Dīpāvalī **Madhusudan Mishra**
1.11.2005

Preface

Contents

Introduction

The Santhali language, or Santhali, is the northern branch of the so-called Munda group of languages. This group is said to comprise the following dialects: Kharwari, Mundari, Ho, Birhor, Kurku, Ka, Semang, Khmer, Bahnar, Stieng, Churu, Chong, Tareng, Sue, Halang, Alok, Mon, and, possibly, some others.

It is a primitive type of language, at least in the sense that the same word can be used as all parts of speech and, typologically, it is agglutinative. Its little clauses can be appropriately compared with Swahili clauses:

Swahili	*Santhali*
a-li-ku-ona	sen-ket-ā-e
he-past-you-see	go-past-he
(He saw you)	(He went)

It is said to differ from the socalled Aryan group of the analytic languages on the one hand and from the socalled Dravidian group of the agglutinative languages on the other. Before the coming of the Christian missionaries in this tribal belt of India, the Munda dialects, like the village dialects of the whole of India, were never taken into account. The people speaking these dialects were not considered to be of a different human stock, because they are known to be fully conversant with the Hindu tradition and its language. It was only the European scholars who taught us to distinguish among the three groups of the Indian languages and the people speaking them.

As we shall see in course of this book, this distinction is superficial and fabricated, because the bush of all the Indian languages has a single root under the earth, many common morphological elements of which have been effaced in course of its long history.

A word-by-word paraphrasing of a Santhali sentence in any Indian language is almost parallel, which shows its common ancestry.

For example:

sabūd menak-t-am-a noa kathā reak
sabūt hä terā is bāt kā ?
(Have you any proof of this fact ?)

Every state of India has its socalled state language, also called provincial or regional language, namely:

Assamese	Assam
Bengali	Bengal
Oriya	Orissa
Gujarati	Gujarat
Marathi	Maharashtra
Punjabi	Punjab
Kashmiri	Kashmir
Dogri	Jammu
Manipuri	Manipur
Tamil	Tamil Nadu
Telugu	Andhra
Malayalam	Kerala
Kannad	Karnataka

Though the Sindhi language has no separate state in India, its speakers are there in a large number. Even

Nagaland, Mizoram, Arunachal and Meghalaya have their respective languages, split into various dialects. Other states, namely Bihar, Uttar Pradesh, Madhya Pradesh, Rajasthan, Haryana, Himachal Pradesh, and their recent off-shoots have Hindi as the official state language. It does not, however, mean that they have no languages of their own.

Under the dominance of the state languages, and specifically of the migrant Hindi, there are smaller regional dialects with separate names, some of them having rich literature of their own. Though differing morphologically and vocabulary-wise in their details, they have surprising similarity at the bottom. Typologically they are agglutinative, though Hindi and other state languages outside the Dravidian region are analytic, descending from the synthetic inflexional ancestor.

There should have been a common Bihari language like Oriya and Bengali, but the natural boundaries created by the massive rivers in Bihar split it into three major dialects, namely: Maithili (now a fully literary language with rich literature), Bhojpuri (also having some amount of literature) and Magahi (only recently coming into writing and having no literary documents). They are covered atop by Hindi, migrating from the western region. Even new regional dialects within these three, namely Bajjikā, Angikā, Nāgpuri and others from the other areas of the Hindi states, though having outer differences, are remarkably similar at bottom.

A comparison of these regional dialects of the Hindi states with the dialects of the Munda group shows that, apart from their coming under the same geography, they are cousins and go to a common ancestor.

The Bihari dialects show the plurality of the subject and object agglutinatively like Santhali, not through inflexion like Hindi. Of course, the affixing elements are different in Santhali and in the Bihari dialects. For example:

Santhali	hor (a man)	sg.	hor-ko	pl.
Bihari	maugī (woman)	sg.	maugī-sa	pl.
Hindi	kitāb (a book)	sg.	kitāb-ẽ	pl.

While taking postpositions, the Hindi forms bend further: kitāb-õ mẽ (in books). There is no such bending in Santhali and in the Bihari dialets: hor-ko-reak, maugī-sa-ke, etc.

Due to some remarkable social differences, the Bihari dialects have three distinct layers in verbs in the 2nd person imperative:

Polite	:	jā-ū (please go), kah-ū (please tell)
Normal	:	jā (go !) kah-a (tell !)
Rude	:	j-o (go !) kah (tell !)

The Santhali form is just one for all persons in every tense and mood, because the sharp social differences are not known to them.

In the Bihari dialects, on the other hand, the 1st and 2nd person polite forms in the verbs and pronouns are the same. Some of the Bihari dialects distinguish gender also in verbs, because the influence of Sanskrit has been tremendous even in ordinary life. They are different from Hindi in not having a changeable ā adjective: choṭā baccā

m. (a little child), chote bacce pl., choṭe bacce se postpositional sg. chote bacc-õ se ppl. pl. choṭī baccī f. Other-wise, the adjective is neutral in Hindi also, becase it does not bend like nouns and pronouns. In the Bihari dialects, the adjective choṭ is always the same. Hindi, of the inflexional parentage, has little paradigms of declension and conjugation. The Bihari dialects typically follow Santhali, except that the cultivated Maithili and Bhojpuri distinguish genders in verbs in polite expression: gelāh m. gelīh f. and gail-an m. gailī f. (= He went, she went).

It can be confidently said that the regional dialects of some Hindi states, specially of Bihar, are cognate with Santhali and belong to the eastern group of languages. They should be called the eastern dialects, the Dravidian being the southern and the Aryan being the north-western dialects. Before the coming of Hindi from the western region and spreading over these dialects as the medium of instruction in schools, a large quantity of the Santhal vocabulary was in use among the uneducated villagers. As the village dialects have been becoming unpopular by the introduction of Hindi, the old vocabulary has gone to the remote villages where there are no schools. Even then some Santhal verbs like agdhāo (to boast, be fastidious), dāg (to burn) have entered the local Hindi vocabulary. As a matter of fact, the local Hindi in every region has been influenced by the regional dialects. In Bihari Hindi, the passive ne is hardly spoken. They say: ham kah-e for mā̃ne kah-ā (I said).

Briefly, it can be said that the village dialects should not be associated with Hindi of the inflexional lineage. The migration of Hindi towards the east has pushed the Santhali vocabulary to the tribal belt. Morphologically, the Bihari dialects have nothing to do with Hindi of the inflexional lineage, because they belong to the eastern group of the agglutinative languages.

The linguistic researches of the last century: the evolution of Māgadhī by Banerjee-Shastri, the evolution of Awadhi by B.R. Saxena, La langue Braja by Dhirendra Verma, the evolution of Bhojpuri by Bishwanath Prasad, and the origin and development of Maithili by Subhadra Jha—never thought of the cognateness of these dialects with the Munda group, and they have been treated as in direct lineage of the inflexional languages. Subhadra Jha referred to some non-IE elements in Maithili, which were traced by a reviewer in the Santhal dictionary. Even then the Aryan relationship of Maithili and other dialects of the Hindi states is taken to be absolutely doubtless. It is rather thought to be disparaging, if these dialects are said to be related with Santhali in morphology.

The modern Indian linguistic research under the direct supervision of the European linguists has remained so much unilateral that every element in the north Indian dialects seems to reflect in Sanskrit and unusual elements are said to be borrowing.

This idea of the existence of three distinct linguistic families inside India has played havoc academically and no one is prepared to think of the common origin of the Indian languages. Grierson's linguistic survey of India has badly distorted the Indian ethnology. First of all, there was a linguistic division into Aryan, Dravidian and Munda; then the people speaking these languages were called Aryan, Dravidian and Austric.

The unfathomable antiquities of India and the disbelief in its real documents, namely itihāsa and purāṇa texts, has easily given way to the fabricated history. Apart from the fact that its real witness is still said to be dumb, a group of historians take pride in believing in the invasion which never was. But now the invasion-theory has become unpopular among them too, and a new term acculturation has been coined.

The linguistic differences can be accounted for by the loss of contact between the two groups of the same people, but to think of separate races on this basis is a sin. If this distinction was guided by some mischievous thinking, that should now be exposed. The British reconstruction of the Indian history is the result of the zeal of the Christian missionaries, and there is only a little scholarship in it.

India is a country of cities and villages, which differ culturally like day and night. The cities are inhabited by the multi racial, multi-cultural and multi-social groups, while each village is inhabited by a special group of people. Therefore, there are sometimes village dialects. Often, in the same big village two different communities speak two different dialects. Apart from this, there are some regions of twilight, where a mixed language has sprung up. In such an uneven social geography of the country, the linguistic survey of Grierson has tumbled down.

We can say, the Indian society has upper and lower levels of speech throughout the country. The upper level of speech is sophisticated, analytic in the north and agglutinative in the south. The analytic languages have descended from the synthetic-inflexional ancestor, themselves having some amount of inflexion. Though the agglutinative language of the upper level has no inflexional background, its capacity to borrow words and expression from the foreign sources is excellent, which has distanced it from the same of the lower level. Thus the agglutinative languages too have at least two layers. The agglutinative languages of the higher and lower levels do not differ morphologically but in vocabulary and modes of expression.

Though the linguistic contact between north and south in India, after the catastrophic separation in the midnight of the history, began at the stage of the socalled middle Indo-Aryan, later there was an influx of the Sanskrit vocabulary in the southern languages, so that the middle Indic has been naturalized by the Dravidian languages. For example, kṛṣṇa entered Tamil through the Prakrit kaṇha and was naturalized as kanna-n before kṛṣṇa was bodily taken to that language.

The language should have been identified level-wise, and then grouped morphologically. But according to Grierson's survey, even Maithili is analytic, of the inflexional parentage, which it is not. It is typically agglutinative like all other Bihari dialects. The Maithili speaking people are intimately related with the Vedic tradition, but they speak an agglutinative language. It was never considered while undertaking the linguistic survey.

As a matter of fact, the socalled Aryan, Dravidian and Munda groups of languages, having no inhibition about borrowing among themselves, go to a common source. But because the modern Aryan languages of India show their descent from the inflexional ancestor, also themselves having some amount of inflexion, and also because the

Dravidian and Munda groups do not show any sign of their descent from the inflexional ancestor, typologically being agglutinative, the common ancestry of the three groups of languages is seriously doubted. The three groups of languages are not at the three angles of the triangle but on their arms, at unequal distances on account of varying speed of development.

It may be supposed that the ancestors of the Aryan, Dravidian and Munda groups of languages separated at the very early phase of the agglutinative stage. That is to say, at the end of the isolating stage of the ancestor, the languages branched in V-shape due to some natural catastrophe, onc arm reaching the inflexional stage but the other dwarfed by breaking into two and remaining limping at the same stage. When Sanskrit was analysed as the inflexional language, Tamil was analysed as an agglutinative language on the same latitude of the history. We can imagine the period of the common agglutinative parent and its isolating parent (that is, the grand-parent).

That is to say, the Aryan group reached the inflexional stage. But the ancestors of the modern Munda and Dravidian groups remained limping at the agglutinative stage without any contact with each other. Though we have no records to prove, the Tamil and Munda languages are older than Sanskrit. And the village dialects of the whole of India go to a remote antiquity, being older than Sanskrit, suffering little or no change.

At the agglutinative stage or slightly earlier, all the Indian languages were one. Either all of them are Dravidian or all of them are Aryan. The austric is a ghost idea. Whereas the north Indian languages are analytic (a mixture of isolating, agglutinative and inflexional), the regional dialects are agglutinative like the Munda and Dravidian groups of languages. It means that even when one arm of the V reached the inflexional stage, its core or the agglutinative form remained buried under its feet and limped on. Even Maithili, the champion of the Vedic tradition, is typically agglutinative.

Burrow-Emeneau's Dravidian etymological dictionary compares the common Dravidian words with Sanskrit and Bodding's Santhal dictionary compares the Santhal and Munda words with those of Hindi, Bengali, Oriya and Bihari. But even a triangular comparison of Dravidian, Munda and Aryan vocabulary is possible. There are pockets of Dravidian in Munda and Aryan regions, just as there are at present pockets of Oriya speaking people in Mithila and of Maithili speaking people in the Bhojpuri area. Some Kannad and Telugu speaking groups of people came to Mithila and were completely merged in the local population with high social status.

A comparative and etymological dictionary and, ultimately, a similar grammar of Dravidian, Munda and Aryan groups may bring to light the common elements which may lead to their common ancestor. But this chapter of the common ancestry may be closed here for the rest of the book.

The Santhali grammar itself will now speak how it is not only nearer but akin to the Bihari dialects, which have nothing to do with the inflexional lineage. The Bihari dialects are gloriously agglutinative, having no trace of the inflexional ancestor.

The present grammar of the Santhal language is exclusively based on the linguistic material of Bodding's Santhal dictionary. The common morphological elements of Santhali and Bihari dialects have been highlighted everywhere. Though the ancestors of the three groups of languages separated at the early phase of the agglutinative stage, there are a few common elements visible in their forms. The e- in e-ka (one) is not different from e- in Tamil el̲u (seven), but the numerals changed drastically in both the languages at some period in their history. The dental -t- is one of the typical elements attached to 3p.sg. of the verb. In Sanskrit and cognate languages it has spread over the whole conjugational system as regards the 3p.sg. But in Santhali, where there is no distinction of number and person in the verb, it is the only surviving element. Perhaps they had separated at a time when the 3p.sg. in verbs had been clearly distinguished. Let us compare Sanskrit, Tamil, Bihari and Santhali:

cal-a-ti	van-t-ān̲	cal-at-ā	calao-et-ā
(He goes)	(He came)	(He goes)	(He goes)
a-cal-a-t	pārt-t-ān̲	calait-achi -bā -ha	calao-ket-a
(He went)	(He saw)	etc.	(He went)

This single morphological element is enough to show the cognateness of the Aryan, Dravidian and Munda groups of languages. We must ignore the typical features of the different languages.

The identical syllabary, a rare morphological element and the parallel sentence pattern are proofs for the common origin of all the Indian languages. The writing of the Santhali grammar has given an insight into the mischief played by the scholarship of the religious bigotry.

1

The Sounds of Santhali

1. The Santhal language has the following vowels and consonants:

(a) Vowels

Simple	:	a ā	i ī	u ū	ĕ e	ŏ o
Diphthongs	:	ai	au	ae	ao	

The vowel a is closed, = u in cup, but the vowel ā is open, both short and long.

Though these vowels are comparable to those of the Bihari dialects, the Santhali vowels are often shorter, whereas the same in the Bihari dialects are long. Because e and o are generally written and pronounced long, their short forms are indicated by ĕ and ŏ.

The vowels are also nasalised with their short and long forms; e.g. ã, ũ̄, etc.

(b) Consonants

The consonants are distinguished as stops and fricatives as well as voiceless and voiced, the stops also distinguished as plain, aspirates and nasals.

Voiceless			Voiced		
Stops	plain	aspirate	plain	aspirate	nasal
Velar	k	kh	g	gh	ṅ
Palatal	c	ch	j	jh	ñ
Cerebral	ṭ	ṭh	ḍ	ḍh	ṇ
Dental	t	th	d	dh	n
Labial	p	ph	b	bh	m
Fricatives					
Palatal				y	
Cerebral				r	
Dental		s		l	
Dento-labial				v	
Velar				h	

The sound h is voiceless and voiced only in pronunciation, not in writing. In certain dialects, the voiceless h is silent, in certain others represented by k.

The dento-labial v is sometimes the bilabial w.

There is no Anusvār or Visarg, which are carried in Hindi and Bihari dialects through the Sanskrit words, but never correctly pronounced.

The original ḍ and ḍh are pronounced as flap sounds ṛ and ṛh between two vowels and at the end of a word in Santhali. But they have also arisen independently.

2. Phonetic Peculiarities

Santhali has some phonetic peculiarities, which are specially to be taken note of.

(a) There is interchange between e and a in the same word:

banāo : benāo (make)
an-ā : en-ā (is, are)

at : et (affix)
kat : ket (affix)

(b) The non-Santhali long vowels are pronounced short in Santhali:

vināś : vinas (destruction)
hāthī : hatī (elephant)
māṭī : maṭī (earth)

(c) The Santhali l generally corresponds to r in the Bihari dialects:

kārīgar : kārīgol (artisan)
dohrānā: dohlāo (repeat)
mandir : mandil (temple)

(d) The aspirates of the Bihari dialects are often represented by the plain stops, and voicing also is lost:

māf : māp (forgive)
lābh : lāp (gain)
rath : rat (car)
dukh : duk (sorrow)
dhamkānā : domkāo (scold)
ādhā : ādā (half)

(e) The non-Santhali n appears as l in Santhali:

naukā : laukā (boat)
nālis : lālis (complain)
nāgarī : lāgrī (the script)

This change of n to r and l is attested by Pāṇini:

śarvan + ī : śarvar-ī (night)

(f) The Santhali a is written and pronounced as the Bengali a; e.g. man (mind) – mon, dhan (wealth) – dhon, etc.

(g) Santhali has assimilated all the foreign sounds in its syllabary. Thus ś, f, z, <u>gh</u>, etc. are unknown to the Santhali syllabary, all replaced by s, ph, j, g, etc, if such words are borrowed.

This is actually the state of affairs in all the Bihari dialects. But because they have the Sanskrit and Hindi influence in their cultural life, they write the foreign words as far as accommodated by Nāgarī. However, they are hardly pronounced as such.

3. Sandhi

Bodding has presented the sentences of Santhali from the actually spoken language. Therefore, the words when seen in their individual capacity, exhibit typical features of Sandhi, not generally found in the modern languages.

(a) Two similar vowels merge together as single (long) vowels:

ba (not) + am (you) = bām
idi (take) + ia (anything) = idīa
jumi (field) + iñ (I) = jumīñ (my land)

(b) After an u, the following e is reduced to i:

agu (bring) + e (it)-pe = agu-i-pe
bahū (bride) + e= bahu-i

(c) The radical or infixal final c, k, t, p are voiced to j g d b respectively:

dec + ok = dej-ok

māk + re = māg-re
ket + e-a = ked-e-a
sap + me = sab-me

(d) The vowel a at the beginning of a word is dropped after e o at the end of a word:

ge + añ = geñ
do + am = dom
oṛak-re + añ = oṛak-re-ñ

(e) After a word ending with a vowel, often -y- is inserted before e and -w- before a, just on phonetic ground:

hasa (be lost) -y-en-ā (was lost)
hasa (bury) -w- ad-e-ā-ko (they buried him)

Though Bodding has not shown the vowels as short and long in Santhali, I have often done it, if the words are found in the Bihari dialects. As I have no direct access to the Santhali language, I may be wrong at some places, but that may kindly be put up with.

The more or less identical syllabary of all the Indian languages suggest that they have descended from a common ancestor. Due to different geographical situations, however, there are some phonetic peculiarities in different languages: the Bengali language is remarkable though its choice for the palatal ś for all the sibilants and for b in place of v; the south Indian languages have retained the cerebrals very faithfully; and the Munda group appears to be inclined for lambdacism. The cerebrals were not introduced to Sanskrit but were lost from it.

2

The Relationship of Words

4. There are five parts of speech according to the Indian system of grammar, namely: noun, pronoun, adjective, verb and unchangeable. In the western system of grammar, the unchangeables are further divided as adverb, preposition conjunction and interjection. In place of prepositions of the western languages, the Indian languages have postpositions. There are also some prefixed elements, borrowed from outside: be- (without), etc.

5. The nouns and pronouns are either subject or object or both of the finite verb in the sentence. They are themselves qualified either attributively or predicatively by the adjectives. Their relationships among themselves are shown by the postpositions.

6. The postpositions are so called because they are put after the words. They are many, but as far as they show the relationship of one word with another in the sentence, they are the following: e, le, ko, te, teko, tele, lāgit, ren, reak, re.

Now we take up all parts of speech one by one.

7. Nouns

The nouns in Santhali are distinguished as animate and inanimate. As a rule, the action nouns are inanimate, and the agent nouns are animate:

abādak (cultivation) – inanimate
abādic (cultivator) – animate

(a) Though there are masculine and feminine ideas, they are not formally distinguished in Santhali. On the face of the word, it is not easy to distinguish gender. They do not also expose themselves as masc. and fem. in the sentence. Therefore, the Santhal dictionary does not say anything about the gender of a noun.

(b) There are three numbers: singular, dual and plural. It is a feature very uncommon for a language in the modern world.

The duals are indicated by -kin added to the basic form of the word. The plurals are indicated by adding -ko to the same. Later we will see that they are nothing more than the final part of the third person pronouns akin (they two) and ako (they).

sg.	*dual*	*pl.*
hoṛ (man)	hoṛ-kin	hoṛ-ko
ḍan (witch)	ḍan-kin	ḍan-ko
ḍaṅgrā (bullock)	ḍaṅgrā-kin	ḍaṅgrā-ko
ato (village)	ato-kin	ato-ko

These forms are used as subject and object. But if the object is definite (= "the") or animate, they take the specific postposition for the object.

(c) Other relationships of the nouns, in English indicated by the prepositions, are indicated by the postpositions, as shown below:

2. "the" e, le, ko
3. with, by, through te, teko

4. for, to — tele, lāgit
5. from — te
6. of — ren, reak
7. in, on — re

For example:

koṛā (boy) 2. koṛā-e, -ko, -le 3.5. koṛā-te 4. koṛā-tele, -lā-git, 6. koṛā-ren, -reak 7. koṛā-re

ato (village) 2. ato-e 3.5 ato-te 4. ato-tele 6. ato-reak 7. ato-re.

(d) Those postpositions are added even to dual and plural forms: okoe (who) -kin (dual) -reak (of) = of which two ? ojhā (medicant) -ko (plural) -reak (of) = of the medicants, etc.

Numerals

The genuine Santhali numerals are the following: mit (one), bar (two, also barea), pe (three, also pea), pon (four, also ponea), mõrẽ (five), turui (six), eae (seven), iral (eight), are (nine) and gel (ten).

For 11, 12, etc., mit, bar, etc. are added to gel: gel mit (11), gel bar (12), etc.

If the order is reversed, the corresponding decade is indicated: bar gel (20), pe gel (30), pon gel (40), etc. Isi (20) is the highest genuine Santhal numeral: mõrẽ isi = 5 twenties, pe isi mõrẽ = 3 twenties + 5 (= 65). Generally, khon is added in the intermediate number: gel khon barea = 12.

Ordinals, not generally used, are made by adding -ak (inanimate) and -ic (animate): gel-ak, gel-ic = 10th, gel-mit-ak, gel-mit-ic = 11th, etc.

In the Bihari dialects also bīs (20) appears to be the highest genuine numeral. The illiterate old people, men and women, just fifty years ago, used to say: cār (4) bīs (20) ā (and) cār (4) for 84, tīn (3) bīs (20) ā (and) sāt (7) for 67, dū (2) bīs (20) for 40, and so on.

There is also gaṇḍā for 4, and gāhī for 5, as among the Santhalis.

(e) Besides the postposition for "of", there are little possessive suffixes, integrally attached to the nouns:

dādā-ñ	(my elder brother)
-m	(your elder brother)
-t	(his/her elder brother)

(f) A very remarkable possessive suffix is -ak:

isor-ak	(of the god)
okoe-ak	(whosoever's)

This -ak is remarkably common to the Maithili language, which is only rarely shared by any other Bihari dialect: bhagavān-ak kṛpā (the grace of the god), mithilā-k rivāj (the custom of Mithilā). It is wrongly connected with the Hindi postposition kā (kī, ke 'of').

The nouns of the Bihari dialects distinguish gender, but they are never highlighted linguistically, just as in Santhali. The postpositions of the Bihari dialects are distinct from Santhali, but they are added to the modified words.

On the other hand, Hindi has postpositional bases in pl., and in case of masc. words in ā, even in sg.:

log-õ se, ko, mẽ, kitāb-õ ko, etc.
baccā : bacce se (sg.) baccõ se (pl.)

Hindi has also a skeleton of declension in three cases (subject-object, postpositional and vocative) in sg. and pl., which is remarkably absent in the Bihari dialects including Santhali.

The Bihari dialects make pl. from nouns by adding -sa (cf. log sa 'people', baccā sa 'children', etc.). It is not the reduced -sa of Hindi sab (all), but an original element. The postpositions of the Bihari dialects are not different from those of Hindi, but are attached to the objective forms: hamrā se (from me). But sometimes the same postpositions differ in meaning: Bihari ke = Hindi ko, etc.

8. Pronouns

The personal pronouns are the following, in sg., dual and pl.

	sg.	*dual*	*pl.*
1.	añ, iñ, eñ	alaṅ	ale (I + he – you)
			abo (I + he + you)
			bon
2.	am, em	aben	ape
3.	ac	akin	ako
	-e (suffixed)		

They are used as subject and object. They are only peculiar to Santhali, having nothing in common with the pronouns of the Bihari dialects.

(a) The prefixed a- can be taken away from the personal pronouns in the middle of the sentence. That is to say, in the middle of the sentence, there is ko for ako (they), ben for aben (you two), and so on. It appears that the initial a merges with the preceding in fluent speech.

The suffixed -e is always at the end of the sentence.

(b) The other third person pronouns are the following:

noa (this)	noa-kin	noa-ko
nui (this one)	nui-kin	nui-ko
ini (that)		en-ko
nia (this)		
ona (this)	ona-kin	ona-ko

(c) The other relationships of these pronouns are shown by postpositions:

ako (they)	-te	=	by them
	-re	=	in them
abo (we)	-ren	=	our
iñ (I)	-ren	=	my
	-te	=	by me
	-re	=	in me

(d) These pronouns can take any affix:

iñ-ak	=	my
ac-ak	=	his
ac-ak-kin	=	of these two
ac-ak-ko	=	of them, their
uni-ak	=	his

(e) The pronouns have their own possessive forms through the prefixed t- or ta- :

t-iñ	=	my
t-ale	=	our
t-am	=	your
t-ape	=	your
ta-ben	=	of you two

ta-e	=	his/her
ta-ko	=	their

(f) The pronouns themselves are possessive suffixes:

oṛak-em	=	your house
-iñ	=	my house
ḍaṅgra-ñ	=	my bullock

The different Bihari dialects have the same number of the personal pronouns, but they appear to be more primitive than Santhali. They have ī (he – here) and ū (he – there), ke (who ?), je (who), se (that, this), tū (you 'familiar') and ham (I). The important thing is that they do not distinguish number and gender. In Sanskrit, the distinction of gender was restricted to the 3rd person, which too is lost in Hindi.

If the plurality is to be shown at all, -sa is added: ham sa = we, tū sa = you all, ke sa = who? It is not the reduced form of the Hindi -sab, because Hindi has come to the eastern region only hundred years ago. It represents the -ṣa of the agglutinative Indus (in gāva-ṣa > gāvas, in Vedic dissolved as gāv-as = gāu + as).

The Bihari dialects have the postpositional bases in the pronouns: ham rā se (from me), torā par (on you), etc. Santhali has no postpositional bases in pronouns.

They have also special possessive forms by means of -r with some interposed prehistorical syllables: o-ka-r (his), to-ha-r (your), ham-a-r (my), etc. Bhojpuri has a long vowel at the last syllable: tohār, hamār.

The Bihari dialects are notorious for their distinction in the 2nd person pronouns due to remarkable social distinctions. The pronoun tū is familiar, unpolite, also rude with its verb: tū jā (you go 'normal'), tū jo (you go 'rude').

The polite form of you differs from dialect to dialect: Maithili -ā̃hā̃, Bhojp. raurā, Bajjikā ā̄̃s. Magahi uses 3rd for the 2nd person : ī (he : you). Hindi has āp from Sanskrit ātman (self), which had earlier employed the present participial form of 'be' with some strengthening : bhavan > bhavān. This form began in Śatapatha-Brāhmaṇa and hardly survived upto the early dramatic Prakrit.

9. Adjectives

The Santhali adjectives are not very remarkable. They just precede a noun. This also applies to the pronominal adjectives:

noa ato-re = in this village.

In Hindi the pronominal adjectives assume postpositional bases: yah ghar (this house): is ghar mẽ (in this house).

(a) The adjectives are distinguished as inanimate and animate, corresponding to their nouns:

mit-ak (inanimate) mit-ic (animate) = first

(b) The adjectives of the Bihari dialects are neutral. They just qualify the noun. In this respect, Hindi is different, specially regarding adjectives in ā : choṭā sg. (a little boy): choṭ-e bacc-e pl., choṭ-e bacc-e se sg. postp. choṭ-e bacc-õ se pl. postp.

3

The Verbal Forms

10. We cannot speak of conjugation in Santhali, because it is not an inflexional language. The verbal forms are made agglutinatively. There is no distinction of person and number in the verbal forms. They just show the tense and mood of action.

11. Types of Verbs

The Santhali verbs are of two types:

(a) There are original verbs, typically ending with ao, ae; e.g. calao (go), bae (preserve), etc. There are also others like the ordinary words; e.g. hec = come, jom = eat, lūṭ = plunder, mak = cut, etc.

(b) Even nouns, pronouns, adjectives and unchangeables can be turned into verbs by taking the verbal affixes:

abād	=	cultivation > cultivate
abo	=	good > to make good, improve
alo	=	not > to say 'no', refuse
tuluc	=	with > to take along.

(c) The verbs, whether original or secondary, are either transitive or intransitive, which is indicated by the specific infixes:

bahkāo (mislead)

-et-ā	=	He misleads. tr.
-en-ā	=	He was misled. intr.

mālik (master)

-ked-e-ā	=	He made him a master.
-en-ā	=	He became a master.

(d) There are also derivative verbs: causative, passive. They will be discussed later.

(e) Some verbs inherently express question, negation:

cekā	=	to do-what
banuk	=	to not-be.

(f) Some verbs are impersonal. They are equivalent to 'there is, there are, it is, it was', etc.: menā (to be), kan-ā (there is, there are), en-ā (there was), akanā (there has been), etc.

Whereas the Santhali verbs are satisfied by just showing the tense or mood of the action, some Bihari dialects show the gender of the subject through its verbal form: Maithili aelāh m. (he came); aelīh f. (she came); Bhojp. āil bā m. (has come) -biā f. For an agglutinative language, this may be a case of borrowing. In this respect, Hindi has inherited the inflexional feature of its ancestor and is troublesome through its distinction of number, person and gender in verbs:

	sg.	*pl.*
3.	hä	hā̃
2.	hä	ho
1.	hū̃	hā̃

thā	m.	sg.	thī	f.	sg.
the		pl.	thī̃		pl.

On the other hand, the Bihari dialects show the social hierarchy through the verbal forms of the 2nd person, which is foreign to the Santhal communities:

jā	=	(go, 'normal')
jo	=	(go, 'rude')
jā-u	=	(go, 'polite')

12. Tenses and Moods

There are three tenses: present, past and future. The present has a general (indefinite) besides progressive (imperfect) and perfect forms. The past has a general (indefinite) besides a progressive (imperfect) form. The future tense is not fully developed, generally the present indefinite form also serving as future.

There are imperative and optative moods, not quite fully developed.

The Tense-Affixes

(a) The verbs take affixes for indicating different present and past forms, but there is no distinction of person and number in the verbal forms.

(b) However, all verbal forms end with the final -ā: calao-et-ā, calao-en-ā, etc.

This verb-final -ā is really the remnant of an auxiliary verb (corresponding to the Hindi hä, thā, etc. or to the dialectal -ā), which is obstinately retained, except in a few circumstances.

Now we can take up the tenses and moods one by one.

13. Present

The present indefinite form is made by the infix -et- followed by the verb-final -ā:

calāo (manage) -et-ā = I/You/He/They manage.

The subject, noun or pronoun, may belong to any number or person.

jom-et-ā = I/You/He/They/We eat.

(a) In place of -et-, there is sometimes -at- : kahnī (tell a story) -at-ā = I/You/They tell a story.

(b) Before a vowel belonging to an object-form, the -t- is voiced to -d- : kahnī-ad-iñ-ā = He tells me a story.

(c) Sometimes -at- is preceded by a -w- : ña (get) -w-ad-e (him) -ā. = I get him.

The Santhali infix -at- corresponds to -at- in Bhojpuri:

gāṛī calāwatā = He drives a car.

But here the verb is attached with the 3p. sg.

Other Bihari dialects have similar forms:

Maithili	:	cal-wait-achi, -chai, -chī, -che, -cha.
Bajjika	:	cal-wai-a, other forms as above.
Magahi	:	cal-wait-haī
Hindi	:	calātā hä

The final vowels differ person-wise from dialect to dialect.

(d) Sometimes -et- or -at- is dropped and -a is added directly to the verb:

bahao (make flow) -a = He makes flow
bicār (judge) -a = He judges

benao (make) -a	=	He makes
em-a	=	He gives.

In Magahi also -a has exactly this function: na paṛh-a = He does not go to school.

(e) The verbal form ge is impersonal:

eskar (alone) ge-ā-e (he)	= He is alone.
tājā (fresh) ge-ā (is)	= It is fresh.
nakṭā (noiseless) ge-ā (is) -e (he)	= He is noiseless.

(f) The present imperfect is made by infixing -kan- after -at- or -et- :

calao (manage) -et (pres.)		
-kan (progress.) -ā	=	He is managing.
hatao (take) -et-kan-ā	=	he is charging interest.

By itself, kan-ā = is, are : labār (false) kathā (statement) kan-ā = It is a false statement.

We will see later that some other element comes between kan-a.

(g) The reduplicated verb does not take the tense-affix:

jojom (from jom 'eat') -kan-ā	=	They are eating.
Otherwise, jom-et-kan-ā	=	They are eating.

(h) The present perfect is made by adding -akat- to the transitive verb:

ñel (see) akat-ā	=	We have seen
lai (say) -akat-ā	=	He has said
idi (bring) -akat-ā	=	I have brought

If the verb is intransitive, -akan- is added:

hec (come) -akan-ā	=	He has come.
hoe (be) -akan-ā	=	Has become.

sen (go) -akan-ā = Has gone.
By itself, akan-ā = Has been, become.

(i) Both -akat- and -akan- are further reinforced by an interposed -wa- :

badao (appoint) -akā-wa-t-ā = Has appointed.
agu (bring) -akā-wa-n-ā = Has been brought.

In Bajjika itself, restricted to a certain region, there is -l- for the present indefinite, preceded and followed by different vowels according to person:

1. kar-ī-lā, polite: kar-ī-len
2. kar-ī-le, polite: kar-ī-len
3. kar-e-lā, polite: kar-e-lan

There is a proverbial jingling of forms: kahīlen ta kahelan je kahīle.

Perhaps the communities speaking these forms are migrants from Bhojpuri area.

The present forms of the other Bihari dialects are remarkable. In respect of 'politeness', 1 and 2 persons are the same. The 'normal' 2 and 3 forms too are the same. The 'rude' form is typically 2nd person. Maithili typically distinguishes the third person form by -achi and -chai, which is not easy to explain. Perhaps the latter is impersonal.

Maithili, Bijjika	1.2.	jāi-chi (polite)
	2.	jāi-cha (normal)
		jāi-che (rude)
	3.	jāi-a, jāit-achi, jāit-chai

Bhojpuri	1.2.	jāit-bārī, -bānī
	2.	-bāra (normal) -bāre (rude) jātāra/e
	3.	jāit-bāre, -bāran (polite), -bā -biā f. jāt-ā, -tiā f.
Magahi		jāit- 1.2. -hi 2. -ha 3. -he

14. Past

The past tense is distinguished as the past indefinite and the past imperfect.

The past indefinite is made by infixing -ket- to the transitive verbs, followed by the final -ā :

jom (eat) -ket-ā	=	I/You/He/They ate.
calao (manage) -ket-ā	=	managed.
mucat (kill) -ket-ā	=	killed.

The final t of 'ket' is voiced before vowels:

goc (kill) -ked (past) -c (him) -ā -ko (they)	=	They killed him.
dal (beat) -ked -e (her) -ā	=	He beat her.
hiriñ (forget) -ked (past) -añ (I)	=	I forgot.
ñel (see) ked- e (him) -am (you)	=	You saw him.

Before iñ (object) and similar words, -ket- becomes -kid- :

ruhet (scold) -kid (past) -iñ (me) -ā = He scolded me.

(a) There is also -at- in place of -ket-, and it is also voiced to -ad- :

dāg (cremate) -ad (past) -e (him) -ā	=	They cremated him.
dām (price) -ad (past) -e (him) ā	=	They sold him.

This -at- often prefixes -w- after a vowel on phonetic ground: em (give) tala (help) -w-at (past) -ko (them) -ā-e (he) = He gave them help.

ña (get) -w-ad-e (him) -ā = Got for him.

(b) If the verb is intransitive, there is -en- in place of -ket-, followed by the final ā :

mucat (die) -en (past) -ā = He died.
jonom (birth) -en-ā = It was born.
hoe (be) -en-ā = It was there.
gai (cow) -ko (pl) marāo (die) -en-ā = The cows died.

There is interchange between -en- and -an- :

banāo (make) -an-ā = Was made.
daram (meet) -an-ā = I met.

Even -an- prefixes a -w- on phonetic ground:

ña (get) -w-an-ā = got

(c) In place of the infix -en-, there is also -len- followed by the verb-final -ā :

hec (come) -len (past) -ā = came.
sen (go) -len (past) -ā = went.
dām (price) -len (past) -ā = sold.

In old songs, the verb-final -a is lost = jonom (birth) len = was born.

In certain Bihari dialects, it is represented by -lan : janam-lan (was born), ae-lan (he came), ge-lan (He went). However, this form is used for politeness. The basic element is just -l- : ā-e-l (He came), ge-l (He went). Bhojp. ā-ī-l. In Bengali, this -l- is variously inflected for the whole past tense. In Maithili also it is variously inflected: 1.2.

ae-la-hũ 3. ā-e-l. In short, it is a very lively past element in the eastern dialects.

(d) There is also a past suffix -lak followed by the final -ā :

hatao (take) -lak (past) -ā = I took.
jom (eat) -lak (past) -ā = He ate.

In some Bihari dialects too there is -lak : jim-lak (He ate), kha-e-lak (He ate). There is -lā for the past tense even in Oriya: āsi-lā (He came). It is also variously inflected there. As a matter of fact, this -l- form is spread over all the Aryan languages: e.g. Marathi ālā gelā.

(e) The past imperfect is made by infixing -kan- after the past affix -ket-, followed by the verb-final -ā :

calāo (manage) -ket (past)
-kan (progressive) -ā = He was managing.

As far as traceable, there is perhaps no past perfect or pluperfect in Santhali.

Some Bihari dialects make perfect by ha and pluperfect by ra, added to the l-base of the past forms:

gel ha (has gone), gel ra (had gone).

In Maithili, ha has been replaced by the present form of the verb 'be', and ra by its past form: gel achi, gel chal. It has then various gradations of the polite and rude forms. In Bhojp. there is bā for perfect, with its fem. form : gel bā, -biā. There is pluperfect in all the Bihari dialects, but not made uniformally.

15. Future

The future tense is not fully developed in Santhali. In many cases, the present forms serve the purpose.

The most usual infix for future is -ok-, sometimes reduced to -k-, followed by the final -ā :

em (give) -ok-ā	=	will give.
hoe (be) -ok-ā	=	it will be.
mucat (die) -ok-ā	=	will die.
ruar (return) -ok-ā	=	will return.

(a) The form by means of -k- is not rare:

cala-k-ā	=	will go.
bi-k-ā	=	will be satisfied.

It is remarkable that -k- is one of the infixed elements for future in Tamil. Even in some Bihari dialects, -k- indicates a future-imperative idea : jā-u-k na (Let him just go). It is for 3p. sg., as in Tamil.

(b) Sometimes the present forms serve the purpose:

calao (manage) -a	=	He will manage.
banao (make) -a	=	will make.

(c) Often the bare verb stands for the future:

idi (take) āben (you two) ac (he)	=	He will take you two away.
lai (say) aben -añ (I)	=	I shall tell you two.

Hardly anything more can be reported about the Santhali verbs for future.

In Bihari dialects, the future infix is -b-, but the vowels which precede and follow it differ person-wise with polite, normal and rude overtones:

1.2. jā-e-b (shall go)
2. ja-e-ba (normal), ja-e-be (rude)
3. jā-e-t

The vowel which precedes differs from dialect to dialect. This -b- is the backbone even of the Bengali and Oriya future forms. There is no trace of the gā-future in Santhali, which we see in Hindi and western dialects. As a rule, the eastern dialects have only -b- for future, which may correspond to the future infix -p- in Tamil. The Rām carit mānas of Tulsidās uses both gā- and b- future.

Moods

Only two moods—imperative and optative—are traceable in Santhali, of them the former being widely used.

16. Imperative

The main affix for imperative is -me, which is always the last element of the form:

idi (take away) -me
hijuk (come) -me
lagao (put) -me
mak (cut) -me

(a) As a rule, the 2nd person pronouns become the imperative affix:

barnao (find out) -am (you)
katrao (cut) -pe (you)
em (give) -ako (them) -pe (you)
idi (take away) -ben (you two).

(b) Often the non-verbs take the affix, and it is also intervened by some other element:

alo (not) -pe idi (take) ia (anything) = Do not take anything.
bolao (call) -e (him) -pe = Call him.

(c) Even the bare verb has the imperative sense:

calao = go !
ìdi = take !

(d) Sometimes -ok- or -k- is interposed:

alo (not) bhābnā-
(anxious) k-a = Do not be anxious.
duk (sorrow) -ok-pe = say ! sorry.

(e) Another imperative affix is -akom- or -kom- :

batlao (explain) -akom
domkao (scold) -kom
em (give) -kom.

(f) Sometimes -kak- is interposed between the verb and the affix -me, pe :

bet (cover) -kak- me
lak (cut) -kak-pe.

(g) Sometimes the use of the 2nd person is enough:

catom (umbrella) saṛ
(unfold) t-am (your) = Unfold your umbrella.

The Bihari dialects also use bare verbs as imperative, but it is normal, even rude. For politeness, a particle ga is added. Even some vowel is interposed or suffixed for politeness.

17. Optative

The optative forms are made by adding -ke to the verb, followed by the verb-final -ā :

hatao (take) -ke-ā = (I wish that) you should take it.

(a) In some cases, the infix is -kok- :

sen (go) -kok-am	=	You should go.
calao-kok-am	=	You should do.

In other Bihari dialects, the infix is -it, followed by vowels indicating politeness, rudeness, etc. : ja-it-e 'you should have gone' (rude), ja-it-a (normal), ja-it-ī (polite). For the 3p., the infix is the same -it, but the radical vowel is not shortened: jā-it (He should have gone). For 'politeness', it is extended by -an: ja-it-an. Dialectally, even -uk is heard in 3p. For Hindi, these forms are strange.

4

Participles

18. Absolutives

The absolutive forms are made by suffixing -kāte to the verbs:

jom (eat) -kāte = having eaten, eating
hec (come) -kāte = having come
benao (make) -kāte = having made.

(a) When the verb is repeated, only -te is added:

ñam (search) ñam -e (him) -te = Having searched him repeatedly, jom (eat) jom-te = Having eaten many times.

This -kāte is really a combination of kā and te, because in the Bihari dialects -ka alone is enough:

khā-ka (having eaten), kah-ka (having said), bha-ka (having become).

Unfortunately, this -ka appears to be the reduced form of the Hindi -kar (khā-kar, kah-kar, etc.), which it is not. The Hindi -kar is itself the reduced form of the Prakrit absolutive kar-ia from kar (to do), = Sanskrit kṛ-tvā. In the medieval dialects, the absolutive forms were made by -i, reduced from ia (kar-i, kah-i, etc.).

On the other hand, Hindi itself alternatively uses ke as an absolutive affix: khā-ke, kah-ke, etc. Of course, it has nothing to do with the Bihari ka or Santhali kāte.

As all the Indian languages have developed from a common source, the linguistic situation in India is very complex, and the same form may be explained differently. It is on this account that Maithili, Bhojpuri, Awadhi and Brajbhāṣā were described on Sanskrit pattern and Santhali has been excluded from the group of the eastern Aryan languages. Because the ur-Sanskrit itself was agglutinative, the modern analytic dialects along with the agglutinative eastern dialects reflect in the inflexional Sanskrit. Though the southern languages have deviated more widely, there are traces of common ancestorship even there.

19. Infinitive

The forms for the infinitive 'of purpose' are made by suffixing -le to the verbs:

ñũ (drink) -le = to (= in order to) drink
ñel (see) -le = in order to see
jom (eat) -le = to eat.

(a) Alternatively, -lāgit is suffixed:

idi (bring) -lāgit = to bring
galmarao (discuss) -lāgit = in order to discuss.

This lāgit is also a postposition, added to nouns, in the sense of 'for'.

(b) Even if there are more than one verb, the affix is added to the last:

jom (eat) ñui (drink) ār (and) roṛ (speak) -lāgit = to eat, drink and speak.

(c) Sometimes the objective e (him/her) is put between the verb and the affix:

ñam (meet) -e (him) lāgit = to meet him.

(d) Even -ko is added to some verbs:

ñel (attend) -ko = to attend.

A similar -ko is added to the oblique form of the Hindi verbs: khāne-ko, jāne-ko, kahne-ko, etc.

(e) For emphasis, -e is added to the infinitive form:

kiriñ-lāgit-e = just to buy.

(f) Though -mente with ā prefixed is added to a noun, an appropriate verbal idea comes to join them:

oṛag (house) -ā mente (for) = for (building) a house.

In Bihari dialects, the usual affix for the infinitive is -lāgī, generally with a prefixed e- : paṛh-e-lāgī (to read), cal-e-lāgī (to go), khā-e-lāgī (to eat). This -lāgī is often reduced to lā : jā-e-lā, paṛhe-lā. When some verb is added, this -lā too goes away: paṛhe-jā-i-chi, etc. In Bajjika, there is also -lel: jā-e-lel.

20. Present Participle

The present participle is made by -ente:

goc (die) -ente = dying
dec (climb) -ente = climbing

From kan, there is kan-te (having), from akan akan-te (being).

(a) In some cases, the affix is -ate:

ru-ate = drumming, sereñ-ate = singing, dar-ate = running.

(b) The infinitive form of the verb is itself used as the present participle with some postposition:

calao-te = by managing.

The Bihari dialects form present participles similarly: cal-ait (going), kah-ait (saying), etc. It is also repeated: calait-calait (while going), etc. With some postposition, it is joined by -e- : calait-e-khan (at the time of going). This khan is conjunction in Santhali (= if, when).

21. Past Participle

If the past affixes -ket-, -len-, en-, etc. are not ended by the verb-final -ā, the verb becomes past participle, and then it takes some postposition:

jom (eat) -ket (past) -te = By having eaten.
akriñ- (sell) -ket (past) -te = By having sold.
idi (bring) -ket (past) -te = By having taken away.

(a) The conjunction khan (if, when) makes such clauses absolute in construction:

mare (become old) -len/ket/en - khan = When becoming old.

The Bihari dialects make past participles by -l with some vowel interposed: khā-e-l (eaten), paṛh-a-l (read). If some postposition is added, the affix is -lā, and the interposed vowel is dropped: paṛh-lā se (on having read), ge-lā khan (if gone), etc. This -l- is a typical eastern element.

5

Derivative Verbs

22. Causative

A causative base is made by -oco- affixed to the verb:

goc (die, kill) -oco	=	to make die (kill), to have killed.
hec (come) -oco-	=	to make come, bring.
em (give) -oco-	=	to make give, let give.

(a) If there are two or more verbs, -oco- is affixed to the last:

jom (eat) ñũ (drink) -oco-	=	to entertain by food and drink.
sen (go) dare (be able) -oco-	=	to enable to go.

This affix is a typical Santhali element and cannot be traced in any Bihari dialect. The causative base in Bihari dialects and Hindi is made by -ā and some other elements: paṛh-ā (to teach), khā, khiā, khilā, etc.

23. Denominative

As a rule, any part of speech can turn into a verb by taking the tense-affix, but generally nouns and adjectives come under this operation:

(a) Generally, the verbal infinitive form is added:

balbal (sweat): balbal-ao (to perspire)

(b) Otherwise, the tense-affixes are added directly:

abād (cultivation) -ket (past) -ā = he cultivated

(c) Rarely, -k- is interposed:

kisār̃ (wealthy) -ki-k-sār̃ (to make wealthy)

The Bihari dialects affix -iā to the noun, which is reduced variously: jūtā (shoe) -jŭt-iā (to beat by shoes), hāth (hand) hath-iā (to take in hands).

24. Reduplicated Verbs

The verbs are reduplicated with little or no change in meaning:

cet (learn, teach)	=	cecet
dal (split)	=	dadal
ñel (see)	=	ñeñel
jom (eat)	=	jojom

(a) Some verbs change internally:

kali (ask) = kukli

(b) The reduplicated verbs do not take the tense-affix:

jojom (eat) -kan (progressive) -ā = He is eating.

In the Bihari dialects, the whole verb is repeated, but only one affix is added: khā khā ka = Having eaten repeatedly. Sometimes the meaning deviates: mar mar gel = It died as soon as born.

25. Compound Verbs

Generally two or more verbs are used with the same tense-affix. Then the meanings of the verbs change accordingly:

dal (beat) mãyãm (bleed) = beat to bleed.
añjom (hear) roṛ (speak) = hear speaking.
ajo (feed) bi (satisfy) = feed to satisfaction.
ñel (see) at (disappear) = see disappearing.

26. Passive

The passive is formed by -le added to the tense-affix:

ñel (see) -ket (past) -le-ā = was/were seen.
calao (manage) -et (present) -le-ā = is managed.
badao (appoint) -akāwat
(perfect) -le-ā = has been appointed.
em (give) -at (past) -le-ā = was given.
roṛ (say) -le-ā = It will be said.

In the Bihari dialects, the passive is made by -l with some vowel prefixed, but an auxiliary verb 'to go' is also appended: jā-e-l jā-, kah-al jā-. The auxiliary verb is variously modified, as we may see in the chapter on syntax.

6

An Outline of Syntax

The syntax is an important chapter in grammar. After the forms have been built, they have to be shown in sentences.

As a matter of fact, a typically agglutinative language like Swahili or Santhali is very awkward to a student of an analytic or synthetic language. A clause like 'he go-past' for 'he went' is very funny to a student of English. But to know the Santhal language properly, he will have to undergo this exercise.

The normal order of words in the sentence in the Indian languages is subject (+ object) + verb. But in the spoken Santhali, this is generally the case when the subject and object are nouns:

karigol hec-en-ā = The artisans came.
kora-e agu-ket-ā = (He) brought the boy.

But if the subject and object are pronouns, the Santhali sentence appears to run in the opposite direction (from right to left), because the clause begins with verb and ends with subject.

v + s : jom (eat) -et (present) ā-e (he) = He eats.

The pronoun-object is in the middle, but the verb-final -ā keeps it inside the verb:

v + o + s : dal (beat) -ed (present) -e (him) -ā-e (he) = He beats him. [He-him-beats : Hindi vah use mārtā hä]

Please note that the pronoun e (he, him) is known as subject or object only through its position. At the end it is the subject, inside the verb it is the object.

A curious thing is that the possessive pronoun too stands at a similar position: cāl (behaviour) bes (good) ge (is) t-ae (his) -ā = His behaviour is good. We see that the possessive pronoun relates to the subject (his behaviour).

It is difficult to find a sentence beginning with the verb, followed by the possessive pronoun, object-pronoun and the subject-pronoun from left to right, but such cases are not impossible.

A very glorious fact about the Santhali syntax is that a Santhali sentence can be translated parallel-wise, word-by-word, in Hindi and Bihari dialects:

kathā reak suhi banuk-a
bāt kā sabūt nahĩ-hä = There is no proof of the fact.
nui do nul gai kan-tiñ-ā
yah to aslī gāy hä merī = This is my original cow.

The Santhali sentences have been written by Bodding as they were actually spoken. In their fluent speech, two vowels coming face to face have either merged into one or one of them has been lost. This Sandhi-feature even in a primitive language in the modern age is remarkable.

After this preliminary remark, let us go into the details of the syntax.

27. Subject

(a) The pronoun as subject has to be imagined only from the context, because it is ordinarily not mentioned in the sentence:

dãg (cremate) ked (past) -ā = (They) cremated him.

noa (this) oṛak-iñ (my house)
benao (build) ket (past) -ā = (I) built this (my) house.

(b) If mentioned at all, the pronoun-subject is suffixed at the extreme end of the sentence:

kisãṛ (wealthy) kan (is) ā-e (he) = He is wealthy.
kathā (speak) -ket (past)
-ā-ko (they) = They spoke.
hiriñ (forget) ket (past) -āñ (I) = I forgot.

It is for this reason that the pronouns are remarkable through their last consonants.

hec (come) got (quickly) en (past) -ā-e (he) = He came quickly.

ac-ren (his own) ked (past) e (her) -ā-e (he) = He made her his own (= He married her).

(c) The dual or plural number of the noun-subject at the beginning of the sentence is put inside the verbal form:

noa (this) ato (village) -re khūb (many) karigol (artisan) menak (are) ko (pl) -ā = There are many artisans (karīgol + ko) in this village.

It is a peculiar feature of the Santhal language.

28. Object

The object has to be mentioned in the sentence: the noun-object is at the beginning of the sentence, and the pronoun-object, as already said, inside the verb, after the tense-affix but before the verb-final -ā:

hat (hand) -e calao (raise) ket (past) ā	=	(He) raised the hand.
dāg (cremate) ked (past) e (him) ā	=	(They) cremated him.
idi (take away) ked (past) e (him) ā	=	(He) took him away.
kaḍhao (abuse) kid (past) iñ (me) ā	=	He abused me.
aha (bewitch) kid (past) iñ (me) ā-ko (they)	=	They bewitched me.

(a) The object noun takes postposition only when it is definite (= "the"):

Kathā (matter) -e mucat (settle) -ket (past) ā	=	He settled the matter.
kathā-ko ader (publicize) ket (past) ā	=	He publicized the matter.
noa (this) kathā-e lai (say) ket (past) -ā	=	He said this matter.

(b) Even when there is noun-object with a postposition, there is often also a pronoun-object after the verb, as if to highlight it:

kora (boy) -e agu (bring) ked (past) e (him) ā	=	He brought (him,) the boy.
kombṛo (thief) -ko sap (catch) e (him) ā	=	They catch (him,) the thief.
bahu-i dal (beat) ked (past) e (her) ā	=	He beat (her,) the bride.
Note bahu + e	=	bahu-i.

bahu -le ñel (see) ket (past) e (her) ā	=	We saw (her,) the bride.

(c) The dual or pl. affix of the noun-object is placed inside the verb.

hako (fish) ket (past) ko (pl.) ā-ko (they) = They caught fish (The verbal idea is inherent in the object: (= They fished)

sākhī (witness) -ko (obj.) sonmuk (bring face to face) -ket (past) -kin (dual) -ā = They brought the two witnesses (sākhī-ko-kin) face to face. Other Bihari dialects do not know this style.

Kaḍa (buffalo) -ko thakao (tire) ked (past) kin (dual) -ā = They tired the two buffaloes.

It is very interesting to note that the Santhali clauses can be rendered word-by-word in the Bihari dialects, specially in the colloquial form. Of course, the number is highly important in the Bihari dialects and, if mentioned, it immediately follows the noun.

29. Possessive Pronouns

The possessive pronoun is placed within the verbal form, between the tense-affix and the verb-final -ā. It corresponds to Hindi indirect object in sense. In English translation, the Santhali possessive pronoun with the impersonal verb becomes the subject with "have":

khet (rice-field) menak (is) t-ae (his) -ā	=	He has rice-field (Hindi: khet hä use).
mit (one) kathā (matter) kukli (ask) menak (is) t-iñ (my) -ā	=	I have to ask a question (Hindi: ek bāt pūchnī hä mujhe).
pila rua (spleen disease) kan (is) t-ae (his) ā	=	He has spleen disease (Hind: pilhī hä usko).

(a) This possessive pronoun is generally related with the noun subject or object at the beginning of the sentence:

dular (loving) mai (daughter) kan (is) t-ae (her) ā-e (she) = She is her loving daughter.

noa (this) kagoj (paper) -re suhi (signature) ba (not) ñ (I) ñel (see) et (present) t-ae (his) ā = I do not see his signature (t-ae suhi) on this paper.

A Santhali sentence is never tired of repetition of the possessive idea:

iñ-ak (my) jonom-thāni̐ (birth-place) do noṇḍe (here) kan (is) t-iñ (my) -ā = My birth-place is just here.

(b) With the adverb or conjunction of time (khan, e.g.), there is a sense of condition:

digdha (doubt) menak (is) t-an (your) khan = If you have any doubt. (Your doubt being there).

In Bihari dialects, this khan turns into absolute construction with the participles, the subject in indirect object form: hamrā jā-it/gelā khan (When I was going/had gone). It is also used with words for time: sā̃jh khan (Towards evening).

This khan can be associated with Sanskrit kṣaṇa (moment) phonetically, but in sense the Santhali and the Bihari dialects use it more appropriately as postposition or adverb of time.

30. Postpositions

In Santhali there are no postpositional bases in nouns and pronouns, as there are in Hindi, and only in pronouns in the Bihari dialects. The postpositions are added directly to nouns and pronouns in Santhali.

Among the oblique cases, the possessive is very important, indicated by ren, reak, etc. Then te for instrumental and ablative, lāgit for dative and re for locative are also frequently used. Others are rare, though quite numerous. We have been seeing them in the previous paragraphs. A few more may be presented:

iñ-tuluc (with me) e (just) hec (come) en (past) ā	=	He came just with me.
boṅga (spirit) -ko (pl.) -re patiau (belief) menak (is) t-ae (his) ā	=	He has belief in spirits.
koṛā (boys) lae kuṛ (girl) lae ko (pl.) enec (dance) kan-ā	=	Both boys and girls are dancing.
ṭākā lāgit	=	for money.
jom (food) lāgit hijuk-me	=	Come for food.

(a) The postpositions are added not only to words in Santhali, even a clause consisting of s/o + verb turns into a phrase by taking postposition:

idi (take away) -ñ (me) -te = By taking me away.

(b) We may also see later that the postpositions turn past and present tense forms into participles in absolute construction.

In Bihari dialects, the postpositions are not many and, though formally the same as in Hindi, differ in connotation: ke is for direct and indirect object. It has nothing to do with the bending of Hindi kā into ke. The affix rā after the pronominal bases makes object forms, and -r is possessive: ek-rā (him, to him), eka-r (his). This pronominal object form can take any postposition: ekrā se (from him).

A comparative study of the Bihari dialects and Santhali with respect to postpositions may be a fruitful field of research.

31. Adjectives

The adjective, including the pronominal adjectives, just precedes the noun, but does not take any postposition:

noa (this) oṛak (house) -re = In this house.
noa ato (village) re = In this village.
jhal (long) up (hair)
jalia (forged) kathā (story)
jalim (plucky) setā (dog).

In Hindi, the pronominal adjectives change before the postposition: yah ghar (this house) but is ghar mẽ (in this house).

The verbs take the tense-affix and then the verb-final ā, which may contain an object pronoun, possessive pronoun and even a pl. affix inside.

The Bihari dialects follow the Santhali pattern in one respect: it has no pl. forms for verbs, though the persons are distinguished. Moreover, there are only two-fold divisions of persons: 1-2 and 3. But again the 2nd person shows three layers: polite, rude and normal. This is due to social differences in the non-tribal Bihari society.

32. Present

The present tense has a general form, called present indefinite, a progressive form, called present imperfect, and also a present perfect.

(a) The present indefinite states in general the happening of an action in the present:

ba (not) le (we) roṛ (say) ā	=	We do not say.
jom (eat) et (present) ā	=	He eats.
dān (give) et (pres.) ā	=	He gives.

(b) The present imperfect shows the continuity of the action:

dan-et-kan-ā	=	He is giving.
hijuk (come) kan-ā	=	They are coming.
mon (mind) lok (burn) kan (-ing) t-ae (her) ā	=	Her mind is burning. (Please note that -et- is not always necessary).
mukhu-te-y-e (just orally) kārbār (business) et (pres.) kan (-ing) ā	=	He is businessing orally only.
ba (not) m (you) añjom (hear) et-kan-ā	=	Are you not hearing?

(c) The present perfect shows that the action has just taken place:

ñel (see) akat-ā	=	He has seen.
sen (go) akan-ā	=	Has gone.
ḍaṅgra (bullock) ñ (I) kiriñ (buy) akad (perfect) -e (it) ā	=	I have bought (it,) an ox.

In Bihari dialects also all the varieties of the present are widely used: jā-i-a, jā-it-achi/bā (f. biā), and there are various modifications person-wise. For the present perfect, the past base (gel-) is used: gel achi/bā, etc. In Bajjikā, the perfect is formed by the rare element ha of ur-Sanskrit (found in pitā-maha).

33. Past

There is a general past tense, called past indefinite, and also a past imperfect, rarely used. The past indefinite may often be rendered by the present perfect. There is probably no past perfect or pluperfect:

(a) Past indefinite

kathā-e benao-ket-ā	=	He fabricated the statement.
noa kathā-e lai-ket-ā	=	He told this matter.
jom-more-kat-ā-e	=	He ate everything (more shows disgust).
ñel-ked-e (him) am (you)	=	Did you see him?
nehāl -ked-iñ (me) am (you)	=	You have favoured me.
ba (not) ñ (I) bujhau (understand) -lak-ā	=	I did not understand.
patiau (believe) en (past) ā	=	He believed.
em (give) ad (past) e (him) ā	=	He gave him.
calao (go) len (past) ā-e (he)	=	He went.

(b) The past imperfect is rarely used:

ñel (see) ket (past) kan (-ing) ā = He was seeing.

There is no pluperfect in Santhali as far as traceable in the Santhal dictionary. But all the varieties of the past tense are freely used in all the dialects of Bihari. The ra-element for pluperfect in Bijjikā is as old as ur-Sanskrit (Vedic kucara, Pāṇini's secondary suffix -cara). As already said, the Bihari dialects distinguish only 1-2 and 3 persons in verbs, but the 2nd person has at least three layers: polite, normal and rude: gel-e (rude) gel-a (normal) gel-ī/ahũ (= you went). The polite forms differ from dialect to dialect.

34. Future

The future forms are very rare in Santhali.

jom (eat) abo (we)	=	We shall eat.
tobe pe lai-ā	=	Then only you will say.
bahu (bride) ñ (I) ña (get) -w-ae (him) ā	=	I shall get him a wife.
ba (not) m (you) patiau (believe) -k-ā	=	You will not believe.

In the Bihari dialects the future forms are freely used. The 1-2 persons are characterised by -b- and 3p. by -t: 1-2 kah-a-b 3. kah-a-t. When the action is directed towards others, -ai is added: kah-b-ai, kah-t-ai.

35. Imperative

The imperatives are frequently used in Santhali. The clauses are very small:

alo (not) m (you) jom (eat) -ā	=	Do not eat.
ol (write) god-me	=	Write quickly.

gidi (throw) more kak-me = Throw it away ('more' expresses disgust). Dialectally, in Hindi, one says: are mare = O dead fellow.

alo (not) -pe akriñ (sell) ā = Do not sell. (The imperative affix is also added to a non-verb).

lai (say) añ (me) -pe	=	Tell me.
kami (work) -pe	=	work !

ma (emphatic) roṛ (speak) -me = Please speak.

Hindi: bolo na !

ma dal (beat) e (him) -me = Just beat him.

Hindi: māro na use !

ma (emphatic) roṛ = Do speak !

(The affix dropped).

mon (mind) -re rebed (keep) -me = Keep in mind.

roṛ-me = Speak

alo (not) -pe manā-y-e (him) ā = Do not refuse him.

aisan (try) kak-añ = I may try.

The Bihari dialects have several layers of imperative forms in 2nd person: polite jā-ū (go), kah-ū (say); normal jā, kah-a; rude jo, kah. The form in the 1st and 2nd person is the same, but the former just shows intention: ham jāū ? (should I go ?). In the 3rd person, -u is also further extended by -k: jā-u-k (he should go). Surprisingly, this -k- is a future element in Tamil, and the modal forms are only little less than a future.

36. Optative

There are very rare occasions for the use of the optative forms:

hatao (take) -ke-ā = (I wish that) you should take.
sen (go) kok-am = (I like that) you should go.

The Bihari dialects have optative forms, but they are seldom used. The main element is -t-, joined by -i- and extended by -ī in 1.2. person and -ai in 3p.:1.2. kah-i-tī

(I/You should say), 3. kah-i-t-ai (He should say). But the final part differs from dialect to dialect. Even the 1.2. form is extended by -ai: kah-i-ti-ai.

37. Impersonal Verbs

The impersonal verbs correspond to Hindi hä (is), thā (was) or to English 'there is, there was', etc. With the possessive forms they are to be translated by "have":

mena (is) e (she) ge (just) ā ato-re	=	She is just in the village.
kathā (matter) kan (is) ge (just) ā	=	It is just the matter.
merom (goat) menak (is) -ko (pl.) t-ae (his) ā	=	He has goats.
ac (his) oṛak (house) -re mena (is) e (he) ā	=	He is in his house.
kami (work) -reak mon (mind) banuk (not is) t-ae (his) a	=	He has no mind to work.
hijuk (come) -reak mon menak (is) t-ae (his) ā		He wants to come (Hindi: āne kā man hä use).
sabud (proof) menak (is) t-am (your) ā noa (this) kathā-reak	=	Have you proof of this matter ? Hindi: sabūt hä terā is bāt kā ?

The Bihari dialects use the impersonal verbs with the dative form (indirect object): hamrā (to me) paesā (money) hä/achi/bā (is) = I have money. okrā bhūkh na chai/hai/bā = He has no hunger. hamrā kāj chal = I had something to do.

The negative particle na is remarkably different in different Bihari dialects: Maithili nãi, Bhojpuri nā, Bajjika Magahi na, often with half mātrā of a. As a matter of fact, na is the central point between Maithili and Bhojpuri.

38. Absolutive

The absolutive forms with -kāte correspond to Hindi -kar or to ka of the Bihari dialects:

thasro (throw) -kāte daka (food) e (him) em (give) ā-e (she)	=	She gives him food throwing.
mon (mind) badão (make up) -kāte	=	Making up your mind.
sen (go) -kāte kathā-e (the matter) suc (inform) -at (past) ko (they)	=	Having gone there, they informed the matter.

Sometimes the verb is repeated instead of adding -kāte: roṛ (say) roṛ (say) -teko thetṛo (obstinate) akād (perfect) e (him) ā = They have made him obstinate by saying repeatedly.

39. Infinitive

The infinitive of purpose is used with the main verb:

cūlhā banao-lāgit-e	=	to make a fire-place.
macṛao (eat)-le calak (go) kan (ing) ā	=	We are going to eat.
khet (field) ñel (see) -le sen (go) -len (past) ā	=	We went to see the field.
khajnā (pay rent) -lāgit	=	to pay rent.
oṛak (house) banao -lāgit	=	to build a house.
em (give) -ok lāgit	=	to make payment.

(a) Sometimes just -a is added to the verb, as in some Bihari dialects: sukri (pig) goj (kill) -e lāgit = to kill the pig. cf. Bajj. māre lāgī.

cala-k-e mon-ket-ā = He made up his mind to go.

kami-e mon-ket-ā = He decided to work.

(b) The reduplicated verbs do not take the infinitive affix: ñeñel = in order to see.

The Bihari dialects use the suffix -lā with a prefixed -e, which alone often serves the purpose: paṛh-e (lā) jā-i-chi.

(c) When the infinitive with -le takes a postposition, the infinitive becomes a verbal noun: cā (tea) ñu (drink) -le-khan (by) = by drinking tea.

40. Present Participle

The present participle indicates the action accompanying the main verb:

gur (fall) -ente gidra (boy) -i thasrao (throw down) ked (past) e (him) ā	=	Falling down, he threw down (him,) the boy.
eskar (be alone) -ente	=	being alone.
bul (drunk) akan-te (being) -y-e thasrao (fall down) hijuk (come) kan (-ing) ā	=	Being drunk, he is coming tumbling down.
patiau-te	=	believing that ....
ṭaka (money) ba (not) e (him) em (give) ok kan-te	=	The debt being not paid ....

(a) If the present affix -et- is not ended with the verb-final ā and is immediately followed by the postposition -te, it becomes present participle in absolute construction:

ba (not) e angoc (confess) et -te	=	Due to not confessing ...
begor (without) lai (tell) añ (me) -te	=	Without telling me.
ñel (see) calak (go) -te	=	By going to see ....

ṭaka (money) baisāu (lend) -te	=	By lending money.
roṛ (speak) -re ko hantao (prevent) -ked (past) ko (they) ā	=	They prevented him from speaking.
roṛ (speak) -te-y-e thalbolao (frighten) ket (past) ko (they) ā	=	They frightened by speaking.

In some of these cases, the -ing forms are rather verbal nouns than the present participles.

41. Past Participles

The past participles have actually been carved out from the past forms by eliminating the verb-final -ā :

jinis (thing) mare (be old) -len khan	=	A thing having become old.
cf. Bajj purān paṛlā par	=	On becoming old.
mohor chāp (stamp) maṭao (eface) -len khan	=	The stamp having been effaced.
jom (eat) ket -te	=	By having eaten.
akriñ (sell) ket-te	=	By having sold.
gidra (boy) -i goc (die) -en (past) t-ae (his) -te	=	Due to his son having died.

The present and past participles in the Bihari dialects are similarly used adjectively: bec-a-l gāy (the sold cow), jā-i-t log (the people going). By the use of postposition, they come in absolute construction: ge-lā se = By going, jā-i-t khan = At the time of going.

42. Causative

The causative forms are rarely used, and all of them are not really causative. Some forms tend towards permission

('I let him go' for 'I make him go'). As a rule, it is causative with respect to the direct object and permissive with respect to the indirect object :

em (give) -oco- ket (past) e (him) añ (I)	=	I made him give.
goc (die) -oco- ked -e (him) ale (we)	=	We killed him.
em (give) -oco- ad (past) e (him) añ (I) ā	=	I let him give.
goc (die) -oco- y-en-ā	=	He was killed.
hec (come) -oco-y-em (you)	=	Let him come.
ban (not) sen (go) daṛe (can) -oco-ad (past) e (him) ā	=	I could not let him go.

This causative affix is unknown to the Bihari dialects. In Bihari dialects the mostly used affix is -ā, but dialectally some other forms come up; e.g. bhāgal (ran away): bhagaolan (they made him run away). Also: bhagae-lan. Sometimes a different verb is substituted in causative: jā (go) > bhej (make go), etc.

43. Denominative

Any part of speech may turn into a verb by taking the verbal affix. Therefore, this formation can hardly be highlighted. A few examples from all parts of speech turning into verbs may be here presented:

ako (them) tuluk (take along) ket (past) e (him) ā -ko (they)	=	They took him along with them.
em-ok (gift) ge bañ (not) at (past) t-ae (his) ā	=	He refused his gift.
bairi (enemy) -y-en (past) ā	=	He became an enemy.
bebhūl (thoughtlessly) -ked (past) e (him) ā-e (he)	=	He cheated him.

In the colloquial form of the Bihari dialects, the denominative is a very usual usage. But some denominative affix is always there. Then only some tense-affix is added: ghegh (throat) makes ghegh-iā, then the tense-affix: ghegh-iā-ia = He speaks through his throat (i.e. pleads his case helplessly). From nāk (nose) there is nak-iā = utter nasalised words, etc. The meanings of these denominatives require great acquintance with the behaviour of the people.

44. Reduplicated Verbs

These verbs hardly show any change in the original meaning:

cecet koṛā	=	a learning boy.
jojom (eat) kan (-ing) ā-e (he)	=	He is eating.

(a) As in many Bihari dialects, even the simple verb is repeated:

sen (go) sen (go) aisan (try) en (past) ā-ñ (I)	=	I tried to go many times.

In Bihari dialects: mar mar gel = Everytime as soon as it was born, it died. Hindi: bhāg bhāg jātā hä = He is in habit of running away.

45. Compound Verbs

The important aspect of the compound verbs is their cooperation in giving a coherent meaning:

ñet (hit) goc (kill) ked (past) e (him) ā-ko (they)	=	They hit him to kill.
ajo (feed) bi (satisfy) ked (past) e (him) ā-e (he)	=	He fed him to full satisfaction.

(a) When there is no tense-affix, there is some postposition:

ñel (see) calak (go) -te = by going to see.

Hindi is full of compound verbs, where the second generally acts as auxiliary:

mār ḍāl-ā = He killed him.
cal-ā gayā = He went.

46. Passive

The passive formation is very rare in Santhali:

uni (he) calao (manage) -et (present) -le (passive) ā = is managed by him.
haṇḍi (treat with beer) at (past) le (passive) ā = was treated with beer.

The passive construction is very lively in Bihari dialects, specially in Maithili, due to its close association with the Sanskrit tradition. The most interesting thing is that -l- is the remarkable passive element both in Santhali and in Bihari dialects.

In present, however, the passive affix is -ā in Bihari: kah (say) kah-ā-ia/kah-ā-it achi (is said), also extended to past by -chal. For the past, there is -l (with some vowel prefixed), but it is reinforced by the verb 'to go': kah-a-l gel (was said). It is then extended by 'be': kah-a-l gel achi/chal/bā/ha (dialectally). When the object is the first person it is extended by -ahũ in Maithili: pīṭ-a-l gel-ahũ = I was beaten up. In impersonal usage, gel- is extended by -i-aen: yād paṛ gel-i-aen (I was remembered). It is also extended by achi and chal for perfect and pluperfect respectively.

Appendices

I
An Outline of the Grammars of the Bihari Dialects

Maithili

Among the Bihari dialects, Maithili is the most refined, having rich and beautiful literature. Though the whole north-eastern Bihar is inhabited by the Maithili speaking people, its most conservative area is Darbhanga with its districts, specifically Madhubani.

The words are distinguished as nouns, pronouns, adjectives, verbs and unchangeables (comprising adverbs, postpositions, conjunctions and interjections).

It has the following vowels and consonants: vowels a ā i ī u ū e ai o au (there is also ṛ through Sanskrit words). Consonants k kh g gh ṅ; c ch j jh ñ; ṭ ṭh ḍ ḍh ṇ; t th d dh n; p ph b bh m; y r l v ś ṣ s h ṃ ḥ.

Most remarkably, there is a tendency to replace the original l by n : pahile > pahine, rakhle > rakhne rahe, anle > an ne chalāh.

The genders in nouns and pronouns are shown by the verbs. The adjectives just qualify the substantives without changing themselves. The nouns show plurality by the postposition sabh (all), although it is not a remarkable idea in Maithili. On the contrary, there is a distinction of rude, normal and polite forms.

The nouns and pronouns show the case-relations by specific postpositions: 2. kẽ 3. sã 4. lel 5. dhari 6. -k after vowels and -ak after consonants 7. me (unnasalised) par.

The pronouns are the following: subject 1. ham 2. tū ahā̃ 3. ī ū ke je se. object 1. hamrā 2. torā 3. ekrā okrā kekrā jekrā tekrā polite forms: hunkā, etc. Other cases are shown by postp.: hamrā par (after object forms). The interrogatives become indefinite by taking -ahu : kon (who) kon-ahu (anyone). The plurality is shown by lokanī added to the object-forms : hamrā-lokanī, possessive : hamrā-lokani-k (of us). Also by -sabh : ekrā-sabh-ak (of them).

The infinitive form of the verbs ends with -b : kar-ab (do), jā-eb (go), de-b (give) le-b (take). This form is also used as nouns deb kaṭhin achi (to give is difficult). Otherwise, it is extended as -bā : ja-ebā-k hetu (for going).

The present participle is made by -(a) it, the past participle by -(a/e)l : kah-ait, baj-ait, de-it; kah-al bāj-al khā-el, de-l.

The tenses are the present, past and future, and the moods are the imperative and optative.

The present and past forms may be distinguished as 1. indefinite 2. progressive 3. perfect and 4. continuous.

There is a set for indefinite or habitual forms, which may be commonly used for the past and present, depending on contexts, made by the following endings: 1. -ī (āb-ī, rah-ī) 2. -a 3. -ae (ā-b-ae, būjhi par-ae), -ik (jā-ik, aba-ik). The same endings are used in the shorter forms of 'be', but only for the present : 1. chī 2. cha, cha-hu, cha-uk, che 3. achi chaik chathi chathinh. The polite forms are the same in 1p and 2p : ham chī ahã̄ chī. The 2p distinguishes also rude and normal forms : cha, chauk, che. Even the 3p makes such distinction : chaik (rude) chathinh (polite). In the spoken form, the final k and h are often unheard.

These shorter forms of 'be' make the progressive forms from the present participal base: 1. jā-it chī 2. -cha (h), -chahu, -che 3. -chaik (abbreviated as jāich), -achi.

The perfect forms are made from the past participal base by the same endings: gel- 1. -chī 2. -che, -cha(hu) 3. -achi, -chaik.

The continuous forms have past participle of the main verb + present participle of kar- + the present forms of 'be' : jā-el kar-ait 1. -chī 2. -cha 3. -achi, -chaik (often reduced to karaich).

The basic past suffix is -l, variously extended. 1. kahal-ahũ 2. -a, -e 3. kahal, kahal-ak (said to me), -kaik (said to somebody) kahalāh (polite) kahal-ī f. kahal-thinh (very polite). As a rule, -al forms are impersonal and passive: mān-al (let it be assumed), kahlā sã (by saying).

The progressive forms are made by the present participal form of the main verb and the past forms of 'be' : jā-it 1. chalahũ 3. -chalaik. Even the verb rah is used : 1. jā-it rah-ī 3. -rahaik.

The pluperfect forms are the combinations of the past participal form of the main verb + the past forms of 'be' : gel 1. chalahũ 3. chal, -chalaik, -chalāh, -chalīh f. also: gel rahi-ī.

The rarely used continuous forms are these: 1. kah-ī rahal chalahũ 3. ka-e rahal chal, -chalaik, -chalāh -chalīh f.

The future forms are known through -b in 1.2p. and by -t in 3p. : 1.2. kar-ab, deb, le-b 3. ā-o-t (normal) a-o-tāh (polite) -īh f. det, kahat.

The examples of imperative: 1. kah-ū, but jā-u (short) 2. di-a, li-a 3. kah-ao cal-ao.

The optative forms: 1. āb-ī 3. kah-ae, kah-auk, ho-ik.

The passive is the combination of the past participal form with the verb 'to go' : kahal jāit-chī/gelahũ/jā-eb 2. kahal jāo 3. kahal jāit-chaik (jāich) -gel achi.

The auxiliary verbs are very remarkable.

Some auxiliary verbs are added to the i-base of the main verbs, some to the -ae base: rahi sak- (can live), likh-i cuk (to finish writing), mar-i jā (to die), etc. da-e paṛ (to be obliged to give), kar-ae lāg (to begin to do), etc.

The forms of the infinitive of purpose end with -ae to which -lel is added: khā-e lel, da-e lel (to give), etc.

The absolutive forms are made by adding -e to the vowel and -i to the consonant: ka-e (having done), bha-e (becoming), paṛh-i (having read), pahīr-i (having put on), etc.

The forms of the verb 'be' may be particularly noted:

1. chī thikahũ bhelahũ rah-ī chalahũ

2. chah, che, chauk bhelah rah-a chalah

3. chaik thīk hoich bhel rahaik chal chalaik

achi thikainhi bhelāh chalāh chalainhi chathi

chathinh thikāh chalīh

Future : 1 2 ho-eb 3. ho-et

Optative : 1.2. ho-etahũ 3. ho-etaik

Bhojpuri

The Bhojpuri area comprises the districts of Chapra, Siwan, Gopalganj, Arrah, etc. in Bihar and the eastern UP upto Varanasi.

The words are distinguished as nouns, pronouns, adjectives, verbs and unchangeables (like adverbs, postpositions, conjunctions and interjections).

The sounds may be enumerated as follows: vowels– a ā i ī u ū e ai o au; consonants– k kh g gh ṅ; c ch j jh; ṭa ṭh ḍ ḍh; t th d dh n; p ph b bh m; y r l v s h. Even though Sanskrit words are used, the same spelling is not followed.

The nouns make plural by -sab, -n : gaiyā -sab, gaiya-n, ĩṭā ĩṭa-n, etc. The pronouns also make pl. by -nī, but rarely. They are:

Subject:	1. ham	2. tũ, raurā apne	3. ī e ū o ke je se
Object:	1. ham-ẽ hamrā	2. tohrā	3. ekrā okrā kekrā tekrā
Possessive:	1. hamar	2. tohar rāur	3. ekar okar kekar tekar

pl. ham-nī toh-nī

The postpositions are added to the object forms of the pronouns: 2. ke 3. se 4. ke 5. tak 6. kā ke 7. mẽ, par.

The infinitive form of the verb ends with -aïl or -l.

The present participle is made by -(a) t, the past participle by -(a) 1 : rah-at, de-t etc. chūṭ-al, de-l, etc.

There are three tenses, present, past and future, and two moods imperative and optative. Other ideas are expressed by their combinations. The present and past tenses have three varieties: indefinite, progressive and perfect. The verbal forms are generally distinguished as rude, ordinary and polite. The 1p. and 2p. are similar as polite forms.

The present indefinite forms have -1- followed and preceded by different vowels: 1. kah-ī-len 2. kah-ī-le 3. kah-e-lan (polite) kah-e-lā (ordinary). The verbs ending with vowels do not take the connecting vowels: ho-lā dela, de-lan.

The forms of 'be' are the following: 1. bānī̃ 2. bāṛa 3. bā (ordinary), biā f. bāṛan (polite) bāṛī f. bāṭe, ha, negatively: nai khe.

The progressive forms are made by the forms of 'be' added to the present participle: kar-at- 1. -bānī, -ānī 2. -bāṭa, -āṛa 3. bā biā -bāṛan - bāṛī, kar-at-ā.

The perfect forms are made by the forms of 'be' added to the past participle: 1. gaīl-ī ha 2. gaīl-a ha 3. gaīl ha gaīl-an ha, gaīl bāṛan.

The past indefinite is formed by -1-, the vowels making the difference person-wise: 1. gaīl-ī̃ 2. gaī-l-a 3. gaī-l, gaīl-ī f. gaïl-an (polite) gaīl-as (rude) gaīl-e (ordinary). Some verbs insert -h- on phonetic ground: 2. di-h-la.

The progressive forms are made by the past forms of 'be' or rah- added to the present participal base: jāt 1. rah-lī 2. rah-la 3. rah-lan, rahal.

The pluperfect forms are made by the past forms of rah- added to the past participal base: gaīl- 1. rah-ī̃ 2. rah-a 3. rah-e.

The future forms end with -b, except in 3p. : 1. kar-ab, jā-i-b 2. kar-ba, jai-ba 3. jā-ī, jaī-hẽ (polite) kar-i-hẽ.

The imperative forms: 1. jā-ī, jān-ī̃ 2. d-ī, dī-h-ī̃ (polite) māṅg-a, jān-a (ordinary) 3. ho-kho, ho-khas (polite), rah-as, kar-as.

The optative forms: 3. sak-e āb-e

The absolutives are made by -ke : sunā ke, samjhā ke

The infinitive of purpose takes -e : 1. likh-e jā-t-ānī

Some auxiliary verbs are added to the main verb : ho jā-l-ā.

Bajjikā

The Bajjika dialect lies exactly between Bhojpuri and Maithili area, comprising the parts of the districts of Sitamarhi, Muzaffarpur and Vaishali, specifically the areas east of Vaishali.

The words of Bajjika are distinguished as nouns, pronouns, adjectives, verbs and unchangeables (which include adverbs, postpositions, conjunctions and interjections).

The sounds are enumerated as follows: vowels– a ā i ī u ū e ä o ao. consonants– k kh g gh ṅ; c ch j jh; ṭ ṭh ḍ ḍh; t th d dh n; p ph b bh m; y r l v s h. Because the language is still unwritten, ñ ṇ have not been mentioned as nasals.

Nouns: The gender is distinguished only through the meanings; the language itself does not distinguish it. The plurality in nouns and pronouns is shown by -sa: log log-sa, maugī maugī-sa. The postpositions show the various case-relations: 2. ke 3. se 4. lel 5. tak 6. -k after vowels and -ak after consonants 7. mẽ, par.

Pronouns: as Subject: 1. ham 2. tũ āis 3. ī ū ke je se koī; as Objects: 1. hamrā 2. torā 3. ekrā okrā kekrā jekrā tekrā. Possessive: 1. hamar 2. tohar āis-kar 3. ekar okar jekar kekar. The postpositions are added to the object-forms: hamrā se, okrā mẽ.

Adjectives: choṭ bar kariā gor.

The infinitive form of the verbs end with -nāi: kah-nāi, ja-nāi, ho-nāi, etc. The radical part of the verb is often strengthened: kha-nāi > khā-i-chi.

The verbs do not distinguish number, but there is distinction of rude, normal and polite forms. The 1p. and 2p. are similar in polite forms, but 2p and 3p forms are distinguished as rude, normal and polite.

There are three tenses, present, past and future, and two moods imperative and optative.

Base	*Persons*	*Present*	*Past*	*Future*	*Imperative*	*Optative*
khā	1.	khā-i-chi	kha-i-li	khā-e-b	khā-u	kha-i-tī
	2.	khā-i-cha	kha-e-la	kha-e-ba	khā	kha-i-ta
		khā-i-che	kha-e-le	kha-e-be	kho	kha-i-te
	3.	khā-i-a	kha-e-lak	khā-e-t	khā-u-k	khā-i-t
		khā-i-chai				
		khā-i-chan	kha-e-lan	kha-e-tan	khā-th	kha-i-tan

The perfect forms are made by -ha and the pluperfect forms by -ra, added to the past forms: kha-i-lī ha, kha-e-la/le ha, kha-e-lak ha; kha-i-lī ra, kha-e-la/le ra, kha-e-lak ra.

The progressive forms are made by -rahal to the radical part of the verb, followed by the present forms of 'be' (as seen in the endings of the present): jā rahal chi. For the past tense, the past forms of rah- is added to the present base: jā-i-t rahal-ī. This may be again extended by ha and ra : jā-it-rahal-ī ha/ra.

The present participle is made by -(a)it, the past participle by '-(a/e)1 : jā-it, kah-ait, ge-l, kah-al.

The absolutive form is made by -ka : khā-ka, kah-ka, bha-ka.

The infinitive forms are made by -e, also followed by -lā/lāgī (= lāgīt of Santhali) : khā-e lā, paṛhe lāgī.

The causatives are made by -ā : khā > khivā, bhej > bhej-ā.

The passive is made by 'go' added to the past participal form: kahal jā-, khā-e-l jā-.

Magahi

The Magahi dialects cantre round the district of Gaya, but extends to Patna and the areas south of it upto the beginning of the tribal areas.

The dialect is as yet the unwritten one, but is supposed to have the same vowels and consonants as in other Bihari dialects, specially Bajjika and Bhojpuri.

The words are distinguished as nouns, pronouns, adjectives, verbs and unchangeables (i.e. adverbs, postpositions, conjunctions and interjections).

The nouns change into plural by adding -an and the pronouns by -nī : bānar > banr-an, larikā > larik-an; ham-nī toh-nī.

Pronouns:	1. ham	2. tũ	3. ī ū e o	ke je se
	hamrā	tohrā	okrā	etc.
	hamar	tohar	okar	etc.

The cases are shown by postpositions: 2. ke 3. se 4. lā 5. tak 6. kc 7. mẽ par. These are added to the object forms of the pronouns, but cf. kāhe lā (for what).

The verbal forms may be only briefly mentioned:

Present:	paṛh	1. ī	2. -a	3. -a, -thin
Progressive:	paṛh-ait-	1. hi	2. ha	3. he, -hathin
Past:	paṛh	1. -lī	2. -la	3. -lak, althin
Perfect:	paṛh-	1. -lī	2. -la	3. -lak, althin + ha
Pluperfect:	paṛh-	1. -lī	2. -la	3. -lak, althin + hal
Past progressive:	paṛh-ait-	1. hal-ī	2. hal-a	3. halthin
Future:		1. paṛh-ab	2. paṛh-ba	3. paṛh-tai, -tathin
Imperative:	paṛh-	1. u	2. -a	3. paṛh-auk
Optative:	paṛh-i	1. -tī	2. -ta	3. -tai (k)

In Magahi, the 3p and 2p are similar in polite forms.

The absolutive is made by -ka : khā ka, jā ka.

The infinitive is made by -e (lā) : khā-e (lā) jāit hi.

II
An Outline of Hindi Grammar

The Hindi language is written in Nagari which can represent many sounds of the foreign languages, even though they are not pronounced as they are written.

Vowels: a ā i ī u ū ṛ (pronounced ri) e ai (pronounced ä) o au (pronounced aŏ).

Consonants: k kh g gh ṅ; c ch j jh ñ; ṭ ṭh ḍ ḍh ṇ; t th d dh n; p ph b bh m; y r l v ś ṣ s h; ṃ ḥ

But ñ ṇ and ṃ are pronounced just n.

The words are distinguished as nouns, pronouns, adjectives, verbs and unchangeables (comprising adverbs, postpositions, conjunctions and interjections). There are prepositions also, borrowed from Sanskrit and other languages.

The nouns, masc. and fem., end with consonants (though written with a silent a), ā ī ū. The short i and u do not belong to Hindi. They are declined in three cases in sg. and pl., as under:

Sub-object				*masc.*				*fem.*	
	sg.	log	baccā	ādmī	ḍākū	kitāb	havā	nadī	bahū
	pl.		bacce			-ẽ	-ẽ	i-yā̃	u-ẽ
Postp.	sg.		bacce						
	pl.	-õ	õ	i-yõ	u-õ	-õ	-õ	i-yõ	u-õ
Vocative	sg.		bacce						
	pl.	-o	o	i-yo	u-o	-o	-o	i-yo	u-o

Many masc. ā words also do not change as subject-object pl., but add some appropriate word: rājā rājā-log.

The pronouns too have subject-object and postpositional forms but no vocative forms:

Sub-object	sg.	1. mã̃	2. tū ap	3. vah	yah	jo	kaun
	pl.	ham	tum	ve	ye		
Postp.	sg.	mujh	tujh	us	is	jis	kis
	pl.			un	in	jin	kin

There are some exceptional forms: mã̃-ne tū-ne un-h-õ-ne

The adjectives do not change, except those in ā (masc.): acchā as subject-object sg., acche elsewhere.

The infinitive form of verbs end with -nā : jā-nā, ho-nā, ā-nā kar-nā, paṛh-nā, etc.

The verbal bases are made by -tā, -rahā and -(y) ā added to the radical form. These bases take the present forms of 'be' and the past participal thā (changing according to gender and number). The present forms of 'be':

	sg.	*pl.*		*sg.*	*pl.*
1.	hū̃	hã̃	M	thā	the
2.	hä	ho	F	thī	thī̃
3.	hä	hã̃			

verb : mar-nā 'to die'
root : mar-

	bases				*endings*			
					sg.	pl.	sg.	pl.
M	mar-tā	mar-rahā	mar-ā	sg. +	1. hū̃	hã̃	thā	the
					2. hä	ho		
	-te	-rahe	-e	pl.	3. hä	hã̃		
F	-ti	-rahī	-ī	sg. pl.			thī	thī̃

The three bases themselves often serve as full verbal forms: mã̃ jā-tā (I could go), vah nahī̃ jā-tā (He is not prepared to go), vah jā-rahā (He is going), vah gayā (He went).

When thī̃ (fem. pl.) is any how dropped, the preceeding verbal element takes the nasalisation: ve jātī thī̃ > ve jātī̃.

Even -tā and -rahā forms are combined to show continuous action: vah khā-tā rahā hä/thā.

The model forms (1. subjunctive 2. imperative 3. optative) are made by the following endings in sg. and pl.

1.	-ū̃	-ẽ	rah-ū̃	rah-ẽ
2.	-, -e	-o	rah, rah-e	rah-o
3.	-e	-ẽ	rah-e	rah-ẽ

The modal form of ho-nā combined with the other verbal forms shows 'possibility' : vah khā-tā/rahā/yā ho.

The future forms are made by adding gā (changeable like thā) to the modal forms:

1.	rah-ū̃-gā / gī	rah-ẽ-ge / gī
2.	rah-e-gā / gī	rah-o-ge / gī
3.	rah-e-gā / gī	rah-ẽ-ge / gī

Because there is already the nasalised pl. form, the fem. gī is not nasalised in pl.

The future forms of ho-nā combine with other verbal forms to show 'doubt': vah khātā/khā rahā/khāyā hogā.

There are various other combinations of these forms to express various ideas: khā-yā kar-tā hä (habit); khā-yā jā-tā hä (passive). The negative passive shows 'incapability': khāyā nahī̃ jātā (I cannot eat).

Auxiliary Verbs

Some auxiliary verbs are added to the infinitive form: khānā cāh-tā hä, -jān-tā hä, -paṛ-tā hä, etc.

Some are added to the oblique (-ne) forms: khā-ne lagnā, jānā, etc.

Some are added to the root-form: khā saknā, -cuknā, jānā, etc.

Some verbs are added to nouns and adjectives to make new verbs with new ideas: go jānā (to refuse to admit), muh lagnā (to talk to), etc.

Hindi is an analytic language, descending from the inflexional ancestor, while the Bihari dialects including Santhali are agglutinative, having no inflexional ancestor.

III
An Outline of Tamil Grammar

The Tamil language has the following sounds:

Vowels: a ā i ī u ū e ē āi o ō āu

Consonants: k ṅ, c ñ, ṭ ṇ, t n p m, y r l v, ḻ ḷ ṟ ṉ

The cases of nouns and pronouns are indicated by postposition: 2. āi 3. āl 4. ku 5. iṉ 6. adu 7. il ēl iḍam.

The verbal forms have three parts: root + tense affix + ending

The infix for the past tense are: -ṭ- -t- -ṟ- -iṉ- -ṉ- -y-

The infix for the present are: -kiru- -kiṉṟu- -āiṉṟu-

The infix for future are: -p- -v- -k-

The endings differ according to person and nunmber. In the 3rd person, there is also the distinction of endings as human and non-human.

	sg.	*pl.*
1.	aṉ eṉ ēṉ al ku tu tu ṟu	am ām em ēm om kum ṭum tum ṟum
2.	i āi āy	ir īr min
	Human	
3.	aṉ āṉ masc. MF	ar ār pa mār
	aḷ āḷ fem.	
	Non-human	
	tu ṟu	a